The Indian As An Enemy

An Analysis of the Indian Question in East Africa

Randolph M.K. Joalahliae

authorHOUSE®

AuthorHouse™
1663 Liberty Drive
Bloomington, IN 47403
www.authorhouse.com
Phone: 1-800-839-8640

First published by AuthorHouse 9/7/2010

ISBN: 978-1-4520-1692-4 (sc)

Library of Congress Control Number: 2010912357

Printed in the United States of America

This book is printed on acid-free paper.

Dedications

I am grateful to my Creator for presenting me with the words of my beloved Martyr Mr. Malcolm Shabazz in my early youth and for immediately answering my purest prayer.

I am devoted to my certain prophet, Mr. Marcus Mosiah Garvey of St. Ann's Bay, Jamaica. I thank him for my purpose. I am grateful to my Creator to have found him in the "whirlwind".

April 20, 2010

Randolph M.K. Joalahliae
South Jersey, U.S.A.

Contents

Acknowledgements

This terse book is an extension of my graduate thesis completed over a decade ago during my time at the School of Advanced International Studies (SAIS) at The Johns Hopkins University in Washington, DC. It was there that I benefited from the tutelage of Dr. Gilbert Khadiagala. As an expert on East African politics and in his kind capacity as my advisor he was an academic beacon to me. He introduced areas of intellectual pursuit and interest that I perhaps will never fully absorb or likewise appreciate. Of course, I am not an intellectual. Nor am I an authority on East African politics. In fact, I have never set foot in East Africa.

The Indian As An Enemy: An Analysis of the Indian Question in East Africa, was actually inspired by observations made while conducting research on World Bank and International Monetary Fund (IMF) policy implementation and popularity in Accra, Ghana. While in the Land of Nkrumah, I came across scores of Black Ghanaians who went out of their way to share with me their opinion about the 'Lebanese presence' in their country.

Bonsu, the man whose family I stayed with for most of my time there was particularly lucid on the Lebanese and what he perceived to be their harmful effects on the 'environment'. To paraphrase him, "Randy – they are no good". Bonsu was a businessman, but even more so a raw, feverish intellect. He therefore, could not help but point out the irony in what the two of us saw together. That is, the Lebanese walking around Ghana like their proverbial shit did not proverbially stink while their own Beirut had become a synonym for battlefield. I tried to disprove the many accounts and arguments I heard from various persons. However, with the exception of a few young Lebanese women with especially attractive bums, I truly did not see "any good". In fact, what stood out the most to me, when I spoke to them about their fellow non-Lebanese citizens, was the blatant contempt they possessed for the Black humans before them.

This, coupled with my constant review of reports on the Arab orchestrated genocide against Blacks in Sudan (janjaweed) and some historical reading I had completed on the Arab caravans and their remarkably violent role in the killing, robbing and raping of Muslim and non-Muslim African men and women in the name of their various religions, and I was led to ponder – how are these people any different from the European agent in Africa? My hunch proved true – they were no different, except that maybe they covered their heads distinctly and managed to radiate diverse types of musk. But they all – European, Arab, Lebanese and yes, as my careful research would show – Indians, considered Blacks either inhuman or inferior humans and therefore rationalized treating them inhumanely and/or inferiorly. And so I felt inclined to take the layman's leap and ask myself – who really are Africa's enemies?

I decided to look at East Africa because I felt that I could be most objective in my analysis by looking into the region which I had – at least up to that point – studied the least. Besides, I had as a youth sat through the duration of a less than intoxicating six hour movie on Mahatma Gandhi, with the Nobel Peace Prize winner being played by the white guy who was the captain in a recent version of Star Trek.

I had also suffered through an absolutely unbelievable (as in unrealistic) movie starring then budding American Black actor Denzel Washington called *Mississippi Masala* in which the main character Washington tried to bed an Indian women who had been implicitly removed from Uganda by the of course evil Idi Amin and surgically relocated in the deep southern United States.

Having digested these two voluminous and equally gross fictions, I was certain that no one could accuse me of any anti-Indian bias/prejudice or even narrow mindedness. Again, *The Indian As An Enemy* is the product of me innocently asking – who really are East Africa's enemies?

While I certainly cannot say that this book reflects any of his beliefs or opinions, I am grateful to Dr. Khadiagala and his then assistant Mrs. Theresa Simmons for their effort in my education. I do not have a clue where and/or how they are today. I do still think of them fondly.

And to Bonsu - se me wua, mensu   man.

May 19, 2010

Randolph M.K. Joalahliae
South Jersey, U.S.A.

Introduction

The history of the Indian-African relationship is but one aspect of the African past
that calls for illumination.[1]

-Robert Gregory

They are an eyesore to us.[2]

-The words of a Kikuyu college graduate
referring to Indians in his country.

"Africans are angry – at their leaders", writes George Ayittey
in his very provocative 1992 publication *Africa Betrayed*.[3]
The ultimate gist of his text can be siphoned from the heavy
words used in the prologue. He says that, "Africa needs an
unwavering scrutiny of its elite and leaders. Concealing or
making excuses for their shortcomings only adds to the
plight of the victims' tyranny".[4] Few appeals made today by

---

[1]   Robert Gregory, *India and East Africa: A History of Race Relations
Within the British Empire* (Claredon, Oxford, 1971), pg. 1.

[2]   A. Bharati, *The Asians in East Africa: Jayhind and Uhuru* (Nelson-
Hall Company, Chicago, 1972), pg.12.

[3]   George Ayittey, *Africa Betrayed* (St. Martin's Press, New York,
1992), pg. 14.

[4]   Ayittey, *Africa Betrayed*, pg. 19.

anyone could be considered more timely and appropriate than this one. Indeed, many of the issues which have drawn the attention of scholars as evidenced by the wide array of literature on Sub-Saharan development are homespun (i.e. bureaucratic mismanagement and corruption).

Michael Chege is aware of these perceptions. In a review article assessing several books on African underdevelopment, he writes:

> To go by the press, and according to many objective observers in Africa, the African continent is in deep, self-made trouble in multiple dimensions-mass poverty, wars, famines, corruption, ethno-linguistic fragmentation, the AIDS pandemic, dictators, even inability to utilize external donor money to cure itself.[5]

In his book, *Democracy and Development in Africa*, a seemingly bitter Claude Ake offers his own observation. "I have been arguing that the problem in Africa is not so much that development failed as that it never began. Nevertheless, elites in power in Africa have had to make an elaborate show of seeking development". He adds, "given a choice between social transformation, especially development, and political domination, most African leaders choose the latter".[6] In a suggestive tone, the World Bank commented some time ago, that "Africans spent more on imported cars and wine

[5]   Michael Chege. "The State and Economic Reform in Africa: A Review Article," *African Studies Quarterly*. 4(3): 3. 2000. [online] URL: http://web.africa.ufl.edu/asq/v4/v4i3a3.htm

[6]   Claude Ake, *Democracy and Development in Africa* (The Brookings Institution, Washington, DC 1996), pg. 42.

than other people at similar levels of development".[7] The inference here would be obvious to a newborn.

While some may justifiably take issue with the source of the criticism, citing the Bank's own well documented and publicized problems with corruption,[8] virtually no one would contest the larger notion that Africa's own have contributed generously to the region's post colonial torment. The problem does not stop here. If we are to blame African heads of state for their constant violations and abuses of power, we are equally admonished to address those who have walked away or simply found solitude in their apathy. For example, the fact that fifty-percent of African professionals have for one reason or another opted to work outside of Africa has not necessarily helped the continent pull itself up by its proverbial bootstraps.[9] Truthfully, does any economist know of a kingdom or country in the world's history that has achieved substantial economic progress and fortune with over half of its professional work force extraneous to its borders?

In fact, one cannot seriously discuss the African AIDS crisis without acknowledging that it is individual Africans and the opportunism that beats within them that has largely left the continent buck, barren and defenseless against the pandemic. The research of journalist Sebastian Mallaby is very elucidating.

---

[7]   Michael Barrat Brown, *Africa's Choices* (Penguin Books, London, 1995), pg. 307.

[8]   Reuters 'World Bank Urged to Check Corruption'. *Daily Graphic* (Ghanaian Newspaper), July 18, 1998, pg. 2. See also Carol Giacomo, "World Bank Corruption May Top $100 Billion", Reuters May 13, 2004. [online] http://www.globalpolicy.org/socecon/bwi-wto/wbank/2004/0513corrupt.htm

[9]   Barrat Brown, *Africa's Choices*, pg. 19.

It isn't a surprise that Africa is short of doctors and nurses: The continent has 1.4 health workers per 1,000 people, compared with 9.9 per 1,000 in North America. What's shocking is that this shortage is partly created by rich countries. Poor nations such as Malawi and Zambia are paying to train medics who emigrate to staff the hospitals of the United States and Europe. We should be helping Africa. Instead, Africa is subsidizing us.

Not just slightly, either. Ghana trains 150 doctors annually; five years after graduation, 80 percent have left, according to Ghanaian data reported by the World Bank. For pharmacists, the proportion is about 40 percent; for nurses and midwives, it's about 75 percent -which is why half the nursing posts in Ghana are vacant. Meanwhile, South African doctors emigrate at a rate of about 1,000 annually. In 2001, Zimbabwe graduated 737 nurses; 437 left for one country, Britain.[10]

The point to be made here is that in view of the dilapidated state of Africa, Africans have good reason to be angry – at their leaders and at themselves.

It remains a fact, however, that "various civilizations have met one another in this subcontinent".[11] As another Africanist put it, "the African continent encompasses a rich mosaic of peoples, cultures... and historical experiences".[12] This is exactly why, after all the necessary and expected disclaimers are put aside and all the political "correctizing" douches and liberal disinfectants exhausted, the issue of

---

[10] Sebastian Mallaby, How Africa Subsidizes U.S. Health Care, *Washington Post*. November 29, 2004. pg. A19.

[11] P.S. Joshi, *The Tyranny of Colour* (E.P. & Commercial Printing, Durban, 1942), pg. 3.

[12] N.Z. Chazan, *Politics and Society in Contemporary Africa* (Lynne Reinner, Boulder, 1998), pg. 5.

foreign exploitation remains an important issue to be dealt with when diagnosing Africa's condition and devising prescriptions for its recovery. In the clearest terms, it is relevant to all who even claim to care about Mother Africa that from 'Cape to Cairo' she has been raped raw and relentlessly by non-Africans.[13]

Karl Marx argued emphatically that history was the story of relationships between the haves and have-nots. Most sympathetic commentators on African underdevelopment have followed a similar path of explanation. They have sought to tell the drama that is the African tragedy in terms of black and white – literally. When analyzing the various scenes, be it the 'scramble for Africa', the colonial drama, the now aging episode of neo-colonialism and even the supposed ideological tumults of the Cold War period, we still see Europeans presented as the dominators and Africans as the dominated.

This project will in no way object to this popular perception for history has unraveled in a certain way as to make it accurate. What this study will do is raise certain questions which at least acknowledge the historic role of the 'middleman minority'[14] on the continent. For example, what do we know about the Arabs in Sudan, Libya, and Mali? What about the Lebanese in Ghana and the rest of West Africa? What can be said about the seemingly infinite hoards of South Asians in South, Central and particularly East Africa? Are these groups, all alien to Africa, in any way responsible for the current malaise on the continent? Are

---

[13] Phrase taken from a text title: *Cape to Cairo – Rape of a Continent* by Mark Strange, (Harcourt Brace Jovanovich, New York, 1973).

[14] For an explanation of this term, see Thomas Sowell, *Race and Culture* (Basic Books, New York, 1994), pgs. 46-59.

they and have they been exploiters in their own right? Can Africa develop as long as they are present?

This project is designed to shed light on the historical and continuing role of these people in African societies. Focusing on East Africa, this book will address the "Indian question". If it does not argue convincingly that the Indian presence in East Africa is undesirable and wholly negative from the standpoint of the black majority than it has failed at its sole aim.

It will be proposed here that the Indian in East Africa has historically operated as an extreme parasite. This statement means to charge that he has purposefully and of course profitably assisted in the prolonged underdevelopment of the region's political and economic institutions.

What should transpire here is a valid profile of the Indian as he operates within the political economy of East Africa. By political economy it is meant, "the tensions and interactions between politics and the economy", as affected by the Indian versus the African.[15] This book does not propose that East African governments start campaigns aimed at decreasing the Indian population or even lessening the amount of Indian influence in its region. Nor does it suggest that such a course would be realistic. It does, however, plead with African policymakers and intellectuals alike to acknowledge the truth – Indians have never and will never share the interests of the black majority. They will never desire to see healthy and functional indigenous political and economic institutions take root and flourish. It is equally forwarded here that if the Indian question is not dealt with soon and radically, any hope that the burden of the op-

---

[15] Robert Gilpin, 'The Nature of the Economy', C. Roe Goddard, John Passe Smith and John Conklin, *International Political Economy* (eds) (Lynne Reinner, Boulder, 1996), pg. 9.

pressed in East Africa will improve is not only unrealistic, but historically and evidentially unsupportable.

Analyzing the Indian role in the political and economic underdevelopment of East Africa is first and foremost a maneuver of battling myths. Generally speaking, there exist at least two trains of myths that preponderate the writings of most scholars in regards to the Indian question. One, that the Indian has played a positive role in the region's political development. And two, that the Asian has played a positive role in its economic development. These two myths serve as the rationale for praising the Indian for having been a positive contributor in the past and more importantly, a potential asset in the future.

To sufficiently devalue these sentiments, the bulk of the study has been organized into four periods: 1ad-1895, 1895-1940, 1940-1963 and 1963-2000. It should be acknowledged now that much of this study, especially as it progresses, is based on the Kenyan experience. However, facts concerning Indian exploitation from Uganda, Tanzania and even South Africa will be interwoven into the fabric of this study to enrich the focus with comparative consistency and texture. Also, for practical purposes, the sections outlined above will be preceded by two very short ones. The first will offer an analysis of the Indian question itself. Some of the major obstacles which have prevented writers from dealing with the question in a fair and adequate manner will be summarized. The next section, entitled "The Origin of the Indian-African Relationship", is devoted to providing an accurate cultural context in which to examine and evaluate Indian behavior in the African environment.

Chapter 1

The Indian Question

After consuming the relevant literature on the Indian question in East Africa and the continent as a whole, one becomes aware of at least one problem within the various approaches. What may be called the question stigma has made addressing the topic a matter within itself. The question stigma is rather self-explanatory. Throughout modern history some of the more unfortunate and distasteful acts have been justified if not inspired by persons willing to portray a particular minority group as a bunch of disloyal, unpatriotic parasites. For example, these notions meshed with medieval superstitions and prejudices, culminated in the alleged murdering of a few million Ashkenazi Jews in response to the "Jewish question" addressed by Adolf Hitler. No less horrible is the systemic mistreatment of minorities in Europe today or the unfolding of the unfortunate pattern of abuse suffered by some Chinese in Southernmost Asia. The bottom line is that whenever people are redefined as problems, it may be expected that persecution will soon follow. It is within this sheepishly conservative framework that Thomas Sowell conveyed his own feelings:

> With or without racism, promoting the no-
> tion that achievement is just exploitation or

> some kind of "disadvantage" to others is a danger to everyone.
>
> Those who are prosperous can usually find some way to land on their feet. It is those who need to develop their own skills and enterprises who lose most by being led into the blind alley of resentment.[16]

Sowell's words roughly represent the position assumed by most persons who set out to analyze the East African Indian question. This is unfortunate. This assumption and the attitude it spawns, thwarts any real investigation of exploitative claims. Thus when black crowds target shops and cars owned by Indians, their acts are automatically described as ignorant and unwarranted.[17] Few people think to challenge the popular position and ask the common-sensical question – if the Indians in Kenya benefit their "needy" hosts so much, why would the black masses who are supposedly reaping these many benefits think of them only as threats to their very existence? And, if anti-Asian feelings were attributable to ignorance alone, why would findings show that prejudice among educated Africans is deeper than among the less educated?[18] Clearly, an honest examination of the facts as they pertain to the accusation of exploitation is justified.

Another element of the question stigma, particularly

---

[16] Thomas Sowell, 'Talents of the Rich Also Benefit the Poor' *Chicago Tribune*, August 20, 1996, pg. 13.

[17] Reuter Textline, 'Political & Civil Unrest; Kenya', *Lloyd's List*. June 2, 1997.

[18] Dharam and Yash Ghai, *A Portrait of a Minority* (University Press, Nairobi, 1970), pg. 2.

as it relates to East Africa is the expulsion of the Indians from Uganda in 1972 under Idi Amin. Naturally, this infamous incident has managed to secure mention in virtually every study done on the topic of Indians in East Africa. Images of the event itself will probably never be forgotten for they were coarse and somewhat despicable. There were after all stories of Indian women being compromised only to be reduced further emotionally by the sight of their fathers, brothers and sons receiving sporadic whippings from Ugandan authorities.[19] One need not mention the many goods and monies belonging to the Indian families that were 'mishandled' by the armed troops directing their forced departure.

All of this considered, it is a mistake to associate Idi Amin and his act with the strong current of Anti-Indian sentiment present within the black community at that time or today. As Thomas Melady hypothesizes:

> Although he [Amin] had probably listened to African complaints about the unjust, monopolistic commercial system controlled by the Asians, or the tales of the continued drain on Uganda's wealth by those Asians who secretly stashed away money in European bank accounts, he probably came to the decision alone.[20]

There is more evidence to support the claim that Amin's expulsion of the Indians in 1972 had little to do with the actual level of public resentment against them. It can be

---

[19] Thomas Patrick Melady, *Uganda: The Asian Exiles* (Orbis Books, New York, 1976), pg. 14.

[20] Thomas Patrick Melady, *Uganda: The Asian Exiles*, pgs. 7-8

argued that what happened to the Indians was not a result of who they were, but rather where they were and at what time. It should be remembered that few people of any kind found an utopian bliss during Amin's reign. For instance, it is often forgotten that Amin kicked out the entire Israeli community almost a year earlier having disagreed with Prime Minister Golda Meir over military aid allocations.[21] The following personal account provides a rueful description of the environment faced by all people in Uganda, especially blacks.

> By the time we arrived in July 1972, tens of thousands of African Ugandans had already been killed in what must be classified as wholesale murder. And we were struck at the brutality of the man responsible...There was something about these deaths quite different from deaths that were brought by a war or a revolution. They were deliberate murders of former cabinet ministers, civil servants, and countless villagers. There were even disturbing rumors about the disappearance of two Americans...A general atmosphere of fear prevailed.[22]

If interested in the exercise, one could construct an equally respectable argument that Amin did not consider the Indian question at all, but only lashed out at them as they were mostly British citizens. During the early post-colonial period relations between Uganda and Britain soured.

---

[21] Phares Mutibwa, *Uganda Since Independence* (Africa World Press, Trenton, 1992), pg. 90.

[22] Thomas Patrick Melady, *Uganda: The Asian Exiles*, pg. 8.

This is well documented. However, while the world's media were taken aback by the sight of a physically intimidating Negro with a less than stellar speaking style ordering herds of people out of his country, few organizations noticed that the expulsion edict delivered by Amin only applied to Asians who were not Ugandan citizens. All Indians who had chosen to apply for Ugandan citizenship were welcome to stay. It was along these lines that Dr. Milton Obote, Amin's predecessor, moved to have all Asians holding British passports leave Uganda in 1970.[23] There can be no debate that Obote's decision to rid his state of Asian-British citizens was detached from any considerations connected to the Indian question. This is obvious when one considers the affectionate position he took with the remaining Indians during his second regime (1980-1985).[24]

The point to be made here is that the expulsion act by Amin clouds the issue of Indian exploitation more than it clarifies it. The expulsion act itself has no certain connection to the issues addressed here. This small atom of the past should, therefore, be kept in its proper context and not allowed to distort, discredit or patronize the complaints of the black majority.

---

[23] Phares Mutibwa, *Uganda Since Independence*, pg. 76.

[24] Phares Mutibwa, *Uganda Since Independence*, pg. 154.

Chapter 2

The Origin of the Indian-African Relationship

Race is the key to history.[25]

-Benjamin Disraeli

The African stands before the Indian's eye
as a person potently inferior to himself.[26]

-Floyd & Lillian Dotson

Perhaps it would be proper to say that nothing incites quite like history. While many idealists deny it, history is a denominator in all inter-race conflict. History as a factor in race relations has two phases. The first phase occurs when two groups with completely different histories meet and feel compelled to draw from their own values and beliefs in order to formulate positions in relation to the "other"

---

[25] L. Poliakov, 'Racism in Europe', Anthony de Reuck and Julie Knight, *Caste and Race* (eds.) (J & A Churchill, London, 1967), pg. 29.

[26] Floyd & Lillian Dotson, *The Indian Minority of Zambia, Rhodesia and Malawi* (Yale University, New Haven, 1968), pg. 297.

whom they are facing.[27] Over time and through interaction and in most cases conflict over resources, the sense of the other is replaced by a prevailing position of polarity in regards to interests. In essence, the format of 'us versus them' becomes crystallized.[28]

In order for the real roots of the Indian-African relationship and the tensions that persist to be understood, the values and beliefs that lie at the center of Indian culture must be dissected and translated. It was a similar strand of logic that led many writers on the European scramble for Africa to begin with a psycho-analysis of the white as he functioned in his native cavity. As one author suggested, "to understand something of the attitudes of the Europeans one must know something of the society from which they came".[29] Likewise, to scrutinize the Indian as a functionary in Africa, we must consider the racist tenets of Indian civilization.

Runoko Rashidi's product, *The African Presence in Early Asia*, is one of the most seminal works done on a topic that has long been ignored.[30] It is valuable to this discussion because of its very responsible approach to and treatment of the race factor in properly describing Indian society. In looking at the Indian sub-continent, the book illuminates

---

[27] For a quality discussion of the "other concept" see: Marimba Ani, *Yurugu: An African Centered Critique of European Cultural Thought and Behavior* (Africa World Press, Trenton, 1994).

[28] For an example of this type of crystallization on the part of Africans in relation to Caucasians, see: Basil Davidson, *The African Past*, (Grosset & Dunlap, New York, 1964), pg. 32.

[29] N.S. Carey Jones, *The Anatomy of Uhuru* (Manchester University, Manchester, 1966), pg. 61.

[30] Runoko Rashidi, *African Presence in Early Asia* (Transaction Publishers, London, 1985)

the pre-Aryan era and contrasts it with the post-Aryan invasion era. It is certain to speak of the original people of the region in racial terms, calling them Africans, instead of the purely anthropological term – aboriginal. These people, known as the Sudra are revealed as blacks and Africans, which of course they were. The invaders, who called themselves Aryans, are reintroduced as whites and Europeans, which they were also. The point of the author is to demonstrate the validity of his claim that the original inhabitants of what is now referred to as India were Africans and to show that the problem of cast in India (especially in the North) has a definitive racial origin.

Rashidi is disagreeing with another supposed expert of race, Pierre van den Berghe, who contends that, "...the Aryan invasion of India, although it probably marked the beginnings of the Hindu caste system, does not appear to have brought about racism". Yet, still he feels the need to add, "some scholars argue that mild racism exists in India and underlies the origin of the caste system".[31] Whether or not one accepts van den Berghe's conclusion or Rashidi's and others seems to depend on how much one attributes the attitudes of most contemporary Indians to their Aryan forefathers, the invaders. The facts suggest that the Aryan invasion did indeed provide the foundation for the modern Indian value system. The following account is loaded with details that cause one to question if Indian culture in total is anything more than a bastard of Nordic elements. Rashidi writes:

> By 800 BC these nomadic tribes had conquered Pakistan and all of Northern India,

---

[31] Pierre van de Berghe, *Race & Racism: A Comparative Perspective* (John Wiley & Sons, New York, 1978). Pg. 14-15.

naming their newly won territories after themselves, Aryavarta, or Aryan land. Throughout Aryavarta, a rigid caste segmented social order was established with the conquered blacks, the Sudra relegated to the very bottom and imposed upon for service, in any capacity required, to the higher castes. These higher castes were the Brahmins, the Aryan elite, and identified with the color white; the Kshatriyas, the military and administrative sector, identified with the color red; the Vaisyas, merchants and farmers, and identified with the color yellow; and of course the Sudra themselves, identified with the color black.[32]

The above social order was institutionalized and legitimized through the creation of a religious system called Hinduism. This can be said since the Laws of Manu, upon which the Hindu faith is based, equates to nothing more than a color codified caste system. The very name for caste in Sanskrit is varna, which literally means color.[33]

This discussion, which may appear as a digression, is relevant because it explains the behavioral patterns of the Indian on the African continent the majority of which are Hindus. It shows as Ghai and Ghai assert that the Indian had a "predilection for social exclusiveness" and racist behavior from the very first day he stepped onto African soil.[34]

---

[32] Runoko Rashidi, *African Presence in Early Asia*, pg. 43.

[33] Runoko Rashidi, *African Presence in Early Asia*, pg. 42.

[34] Ghai and Ghai, *Portrait of a Minority*, Pg. 4.

In his book, *The Indians in Uganda*, H.S. Morris asserts the same:

> In this sense the caste system is of great antiquity; and the details of its proper arrangement in a hierarchy, with the Brahmin as the highest ideal of human life, possessing the greatest amount of sanctity, supported by warriors and merchants each respectfully less horrible, and all dependent in their turn on one another and on the humbler work of the cultivating and servant castes, have been worked out for centuries in the mythological, philosophical and theological works of Sanskrit literature. These are revered in all parts of India and provide an ideal of proper behavior for Hindus everywhere.[35]

Dana Seidenberg is able to provide an even better psycho-analysis of the Indian by including the implications of the British occupation of India. She writes:

> The average Asian trader was steeped in Hindu notions of caste and European Social Darwinist conceptions of human development inherited from the British Raj and supplanted in Kenya. He thus looked upon the African as his cultural inferior in much the same way the white man looked upon the Asian. In this way, he probably

---

[35] H.S. Morris, *The Indians in Uganda* (The University of Chicago, Chicago, 1968). Pg. 45.

viewed the African as a member of the lowest caste and/or in European terms, as an atavistic remnant of the Neolithic age.[36]

This background is helpful in comprehending the contempt which Indians have held for Africans. For example, it would allow us to understand how the great humanitarian Mahatma Gandhi, born Mohandas Karamchand Gandhi, as an attorney in South Africa could share the Europeans view that "the Negro is not used to hard work."[37] Of course nothing in this project will help us understand why Gandhi regularly made his grandnieces sleep with him while both he and they were completely naked.[38] Perhaps this is what the great Indian moral leader meant by "hard work".

[36] Dana Seidenberg, *Uhuru and the Kenyan Indians* (Vikas, New Delhi, 1983), pg. 7.

[37] M.K. Gandhi, *Satyagraha in South Africa* (Navajivan, Indian, 1928), pg. 123.

[38] For mention and discussion of Gandhi's practice of sleeping with pre and post puberty female relatives visit the following sources: *My Days With Gandhi* by Nirmal Kumar Bose; Hsi Lai, *The Sexual Teachings of the White Tigress: Secrets of the Female Taoist Masters*; and Ved Mehta's 1976 *New Yorker* Series on Gandhi and his followers. Credit also to Cecil Adams of the *Washington City Paper* – 2004.

Chapter 3

The Indian as a Slaver:
The Early Indian Merchant (1AD-1885)

It has been widely contended that there was an early Indian presence in the region which predated the arrival of the European. Many have used this tidbit to defend the Indian against the charge that he is nothing more than a peculiar accomplice in crimes committed against the black population. As Ghai and Ghai explicate:

> Whether Asian settlement had begun prior to the arrival of the first Europeans may appear of little significance today... Nevertheless, the point has not been without importance...vis-à-vis the Asians during the colonial period on their superior pioneering record; according to them the Asians owed their presence in East Africa to the European effort...the picture of Asian and European collaboration that such an interpretation gives rise to has not helped the Asian vis-à-vis the African; it serves to strengthen the image of the Asian

> as an exploiter in his own right, and as an
> active ally of the imperialists.[39]

The above excerpt raises two avenues of historical inquiry. One, did the Indian have a significant pre-European presence in the region? And two, could and should this role amount to a reservoir of legitimacy or clemency from the exploitation charge?

In *Kenyan Capitalists, the State, and Development*, David Himbara is concerned with telling "the Kenyan story, and that of East African commercial and industrial development, and to show how and why it was East Africans of Indian descent that came to play a leading role". In explaining Indian success in areas of business, he says that "East African Indians were simply first in the field, having played a merchant role in East African coastal trading enclaves for several centuries".[40]

The focus of Himbara's book is on the post-colonial economic role of the Indian, and it is in this vein that his arguments will be scrutinized later. However, it is significant that he, like others,[41] uses the legacy of the early Indian merchant as a departure point for discussing the Indian businessman of today. Himbara goes as far as to state that "the Indian community is, therefore, indigenous and African, in the sense that the duration of their presence in East Africa spans several generations, and their commercial and industrial activities were formed within East

---

[39] Dharam and Yash Ghai, *Portrait of a Minority*, pg. 2.

[40] David Himbara, *Kenyan Capitalists, the State, and Development* (Lynne Reiner, Boulder, 1994), preface xiv.

[41] See for example, David Gregory, *The Quest for Equality* (Orient Longman, New Delhi, 1993), pg. 2.

Africa".[42] Interestingly enough, while discussing the 'activities' of these early pioneer-like merchants he fails to mention a very significant fact. That is, that the true story of the East African Indian merchant begins with his extremely important role in the Arab dominated slave trade in the centuries following the death of Jesus Christ. This is relevant because as Mahmood Mamdani points out in *Politics and Class Formation in Uganda*:

> The acceleration of the slave trade not only led to the decline of all other kinds of trade; it meant that the very foundation of social production was threatened. In an economy with a low level of technology and plentiful land, the slave trade meant the export of the most critical force of production: living labor.[43]

As one author commented while describing the 'Afro-Asian division', "there was in the background the whole history of the Asian role in modern Africa..."[44] When researching the factors of the historical foreign domination of the East African region, one will notice the necessity of drawing an equation in which the black and Indian are constants and the other member, whether Arab, Portugese, Dutch, etcetera is considered as a variable. This is especially true when studying the slave economy of old East Africa.

---

[42] David Himbara, *Kenyan Capitalists, the State, and Development*, pg. 8.

[43] Mahmood Mamdani, *Politics and Class Formation in Uganda* (Monthly Review, New York, 1976), pg. 19.

[44] Michael Wolfers, *Black Man's Burden Revisited* (St. Martin's, New York, 1974), pg. 125.

In their 1957 work *Introduction to the History of East Africa*, Zoe Marsh and G.W. Kingsworth concluded the following:

> The Indian, who owned a good deal of the ocean shipping, shared in this trade. They were probably the experts who dealt with finance and with the retail trade, for this is work for which they, unlike Arabs, have long shown ability.[45]

George Delf's interpretation supports that of Marsh and Kingsworth. He writes, "Indian merchants used to finance many of the Arab trade and slave caravans in the interior of the mainland and thus played an important role in the East African slave trade".[46] As Marsh and Kingsworth report, the Indian originally colluded with the Arab against the African. What is interesting to note, however, is that even as Arab influence plummeted sharply due to Portuguese exploration and settlement, the Indian managed to maintain his level of influence in the area.

In *India and East Africa*, Robert Gregory describes the period from 1500 to 1840 as a distinct and important era for the Indian. He writes:

> The Portuguese conquest, which began in 1497 with Vasco da Gama's arrival and was complete by 1509 when the Portuguese won the battle of Diu... was disastrous for

---

[45] Zoe Marsh and G.W. Kingsworth, *An Introduction to the History of East Africa* (The University Press, Cambridge, 1957), pgs. 8-9.

[46] George Delf, *Asians in East Africa* (Oxford University, London, 1963), pg. 15.

Indians, Arabs, Persians, and other seafarers in the Indian Ocean…The Portuguese conquest, however, was less destructive of Indian influence than of Arab…After suffering an initial decline under the Portuguese, the Indians' position in the Indian Ocean and their contacts apparently underwent no significant change until the middle of the nineteenth century. During that time, the Portuguese lost their hegemony in the Indian Ocean first to the Dutch and then to the British and French.[47]

The utter resilience exhibited by the Indian community was rewarded when an Arab named Seyid Said organized an Arab renaissance of sorts and moved the capital of his newly united kingdom to Zanzibar. Said is one of the most important figures in East African history. To the Indian, he was a virtual gift from Krishna. Under Said, a new era of Indian dominance began. The Following excerpt explains how this became so.

Although Seyid Said became ruler of Oman in 1806, he did not at first feel strong enough to assert his hereditary claim to the over-lordship of the Arab communities in East Africa…It was not until he had led several expeditions against Mombasa that Seyid Said at last broke the Mazrui power in 1837. Then, having made himself undisputed master of the coast from Mogadishu

---

[47] Robert Gregory, *India and East Africa*, pg. 15.

> to Cape Delgado, in 1840 he took the mo-
> mentous decision of transferring his court
> from Muscat, the capital of Oman, to
> Zanzibar...Trade was Seyid Said's domi-
> nant interest...He realized that the most
> important element in the mercantile life
> of East Africa remained the Indian com-
> munity.[48]

Almost all trade with other parts of the Sultan's do-
main passed through the hands of Zanzibar Indians.[49] The
wealth of the Indian community increased exponentially.
The primary reason was the flourishing slave trade. One
Indian who served as a customs collector for the Sultan
while financing Arab caravans independently died in 1866
leaving a fortune of about 650,000shillings.[50] The Indian
role in the mass selling of black humans became so exuber-
ant that it caused Zanzibar Asians to enter into conflict
with British authorities who by the early 1800's were attempting to curve the slave trade.

The following excerpt is from a report of David
Livingston, one of the most well known abolitionists in
Europe at the time.

> Slaves are a considerable item at most ports
> [he explained] and everywhere are a direct
> and regular source of customs revenue, not
> only the trader who forms the customs,
> but his Indian agents at the outposts who

---

[48] L.W. Hollingsworth, *The Asians of East Africa* (MacMillan and Co., New York, 1960), pg. 19.

[49] Robert Gregory, *India and East Africa*, pg. 39.

[50] George Delf, *Asians in East Africa*, pg. 3.

are thus implicated. It is their business to know every slave landed or shipped, and thus to become accomplices in all schemes for evading the exertions of British officials and the British Government to stop the trade.[51]

Livingston went further with his indictment. He accused the Indians of directly thwarting anti-slavery activities.[52] This excerpt from L.W. Hollingsworth is even more descriptive than the one cited earlier. It helps to substantiate and illuminate Livingstone's sentiments.

The bigger and more elaborate caravans which the Arabs now led into the interior were almost completely financed by Indians. Arab caravan leaders obtained credit from Indian merchants, the supplies of cloth, beads, copper and brass wire, and other articles used for barter in the interior, and when they returned to the coast repayment was made to Indians, either in ivory and other African produce carried by slave porters, or in Mother Theresa dollars obtained by the sale of slaves at the coast…

They were certainly indirectly responsible for the expansion of trade…some Indians had a financial interests in the trade owing to their position as agents along the coast for the Customs Master…[53]

---

[51] Robert Gregory, *India and East Africa*, pg. 24.

[52] Robert Gregory, *India and East Africa*, pg. 24.

[53] L.W. Hollingsworth, *The Asians of East Africa*, pgs. 28-29.

The Indian of today is certainly correct to argue that his presence in the region predates that of the European. However, the legacy of the early merchant hardly allows the Indian to be extended any legitimacy for his contribution – at least not from blacks. If anything, the Indian was vital in disrupting forms of social production (as pointed out by Mamdani) which would weaken the basic economic structures of the pre-colonial indigenous economies. Furthermore, this means that Seidenberg is not only wrong when she says that, "while African and Indians had been in contact for perhaps 2000 years, it was only with the economic impact of British colonial rule that a conflict of interests began",[54] but likely disingenuous in her intellectual position on this topic. There was conflict from the very first days.

The aforementioned evidence, which completely implicates the Indian as a slaver, refutes the ludicrous assertion made today by many that "…the Indians regarded themselves as 'fellow people of color', fellow victims of oppression…" under British colonial rule.[55] In fact, to fully appreciate the Indian contribution to the overall venue of misery for Africans, one need only look at how these fellow 'people of color' fertilized the egg of British Imperialism.

---

[54] Dana Seidenberg, *Uhuru and the Kenyan Indians*, pg. 12.

[55] Thomas Patrick Melady, *Uganda: The Asian Exiles*, pg. 5.

Chapter 4

The Indian as a Colonizer (1895-1940)

> Having found profit either by choice or by chance, the colonizer has nevertheless not yet become aware of the historic role which will be his. He is lacking one step in understanding his new status; he must also understand the origin and significance of his profit. Actually, this is not long in coming. For how could he fail to see the misery of the colonized and the relation of that misery to his own comfort. He realizes that easy profit is so great only because it is wrested from others...[56]
>
> -Albert Memmi

"The partition of East Africa in 1886 and the subsequent opening up of the interior under European administration was to have far-reaching implications for the traditional Indian association within the coast...," writes J.S.

---

[56] Albert Memmi, *The Colonizer and the Colonized* (Beacon, Boston, 1991), pg. 6.

Mangat.[57] It is safe to say that the British colonial effort in East Africa equated to oppression in the eyes of the African. But what did British imperialism in the region mean to the Indian – oppression or opportunity?

It will be argued here that the Indian profited from the British colonial effort in East Africa. Indians who had achieved wealthy status by financing the slave industry were joined by those contracted as servants by the British. These persons, who were bestowed the name "coolies" by their British employers were utilized to construct railroads and infrastructural projects. They were determined to find opportunity in a land where opportunity was being stripped away from the majority. As Gregory informs us:

> Most of the Asians were thus drawn to East Africa by a hope of rising above the poverty level. The peasant farmers, who comprised most of the immigrants were fortunate to feed their families, and many left homes without ever having owned a pair of shoes.[58]

These lowly, shoeless Indians would eventually become shareholders in the colonial economy and imitate the behavior of those who had facilitated the gruesome slave trade.

There is good reason to conclude that the British would have been unable to successfully colonize East Africa without the diverse contributions of the Indian population. For example, one of the major conclusions of the 1890 Brussels Conference was the need to establish a fortified presence

---

[57] J.S. Mangat, *A History of the Asians in East* Africa (Claredon, Oxford, 1969), pg. 27.

[58] Robert Gregory, *The Quest for Equality*, pg. 6.

in the interior of the region. The leaders of the conference declared that the participants intended:

> The gradual establishment in the interior, by the powers to which the territories are subject, of strongly occupied stations, in such a way as to make their protective or repressive action effectively felt in the territories devastated by slave hunting. The construction of roads and in particular, railways, connecting the advanced stations with the coast, and permitting easy access to inland waters, and to such of the upper course of the rivers and streams as are broken down by rapids and cataracts, in view of substituting economical and rapid means of transport for the present means of carriage by men.[59]

In the words of Marsh and Kingsworth, "the conference had stressed the need for railways, knowing that once these were built caravans would no longer be used. It cost two or three hundred times as much to bring goods by caravan as it would cost to bring them by railway…"[60]

The raw labor demand these magnificent plans entailed materialized into a red carpet for Indians desperate for work. The British colonial government in Africa negotiated a deal with the British India Government that would allow for the migration of thousands of Indians to the new col-

---

[59] Zoe Marsh and G.W. Kingsworth, *Introduction to the History of East Africa*, pg. 168.

[60] Zoe Marsh and G.W. Kingsworth, *Introduction to the History of East Africa*, pg. 169.

ony. The actual importation of Indians into the protectorate occurred in June 1895 under the auspices of the Foreign
Office. The circumstances which provoked the formation
of the agreement are noteworthy. Gregory writes:

> The need to recruit workers in India had
> become apparent with the failure to attract
> and retain sufficient African labour. 'We
> began trying native labour', explained Kirk
> who in the 1890's was vice-chairman, 'but
> we found that we could not get enough of
> it...That the natives, when the rains began,
> had to go back to their own gardens for the
> purpose of cultivation.[61]

Fortunately for the British, the Indians were more than
willing to work year round. As Marsh and Kingsworth explain:

> ...the obstacles in the way of its [Uganda
> Railway] construction were cleared.
> Parliament agreed to meet its cost, and
> coolie labour was imported from India.
> The interests of the coolies were care-
> fully guarded by the British government
> of India. It was stipulated that, if a coolie
> wished to remain in East Africa at the end
> of the contract, he could do so, provided
> he forfeited his right to a return passage.
> In this way, the number of Indians in what

---

[61] Robert Gregory, *India and East Africa*, pg. 51.

is now known as Kenya rose to just over 13,000 in 1898.[62]

By September 1903, when the Uganda Railway Committee was dissolved, some 31, 983 indentured servants from India had been imported for work on the railway.[63] To stultify these figures many have felt the need to report the trivial fact that many of these indentured servants decided to return to India after their term of employment.[64] This is hardly relevant if we rely on Gregory who astutely points out that:

> The importation of indentured Indians did not cease, as many have assumed, with the completion of the trunk line from Mombasa to Kisumu in 1901 or the disso-lution of the Railway Committee in 1903. Indians continued to be imported under contract until a new Indian emigration bill was enacted in March 1922.[65]

The above citation serves as a much-needed bridge. Up to this point, it has only been shown how the Indian pro-vided the necessary manpower to the underpinning of the colonial cause. What is more crucial is to illustrate how he - the Indian – actually managed the system he helped to construct.

---

[62] Zoe Marsh and G.W. Kingsworth, *Introduction to the History of East Africa*, pg. 170.

[63] Robert Gregory, *India and East Africa*, pg. 52.

[64] For example see L.W.Hollingsworth, *The Asians of East Africa*, pg. 51.

[65] Robert Gregory, *India and East Africa*, pg. 52.

In his book, *Origins of European Settlement in Kenya*, M.P.K. Sorenson cites one W.D. Ellis. Ellis, while attempting to convey the necessity of Indian participation in the long-term plans of the colony to a superior officer, provided what he felt were three solid reasons for their inclusion. He stated, "Indian traders had been established on the coast long before the Europeans; Indian labor had constructed the railway; and that Indian troops aided in the conquest of East Africa".[66] Ellis could have sat next to one Frederick Lugard, a British colonial administrator, who in 1893 said, "it is not as imported coolie labour that I advocate the introduction of the Indian, but as a colonist and settler".[67] Clearly, the Indian was to be regarded as a bona fide partner in the conquest of the interior and its people.

Indians served in the East African Rifles and the King's African Rifles. These were military outlets assembled by the colonial government shortly after the consolidation of the protectorate. In fairness, it will be noted here that Africans themselves served in various units of these groups. However, as Hollingsworth notes, "the use of Indian troops in East Africa was not confined to the special recruitment of Indians for service in the East African Rifles and the King's African Rifles". For example, Indians who had taken the name 'Bombay Infantry' assisted in the military ambush of the Jubaland Somalis.[68] The Indians were eager to murder. They became killer coolies. As one Indian writer bragged, "Indian troops had come to the country not as camp followers, but as soldiers 'to fight for the flag'".[69] According to

---

[66] M.P.K. Sorenson, *Origins of White Settlement in Kenya*, (Oxford, London, 1968), pg. 165.

[67] Robert Gregory, *India and East Africa*, pg. 51.

[68] L.W. Hollingsworth, *The Asians in East Africa*, pg. 41.

[69] L.W. Hollingsworth, *The Asians in East Africa*, pg. 45.

John Zarwan, "…most Indians were proud of extending British influence and authority in Africa and conscious of their importance and role in the history of East Africa".[70]

Of course, while the Indian's role in the military conquests of the British was important, the focus or emphasis must be put on the Indian as a trader. Again, his role was invaluable because his efforts allowed for the introduction of a currency based economy throughout the hinterland of the entire East African region. So instrumental a player was the Indian that one John Kirk testified to a committee that, "the Indian trader was an important feature", and that, "if he were driven out, they might as well shut up the protectorate".[71]

The addition of the ex-railroad workers to the numbers of those prominent Indian persons already in East Africa allowed for a lightning quick stretch of development into the interior. As Mangat explains:

> While the old-established Indian firms rapidly took advantage of their protection afforded by European administration to extend their activities into the interior, other British Indian subjects were to be directly associated with the Imperial policy to open up and develop the territory. This in a sense marked a continuation of and extension of the precedents set in Zanzibar during the nineteenth century.[72]

---

[70] John Zarwan, *Indian Businessmen in Kenya During the Twentieth Century: A Case Study* – Ph.D. Dissertation (Yale University, 1977), pg. 46.

[71] L.W. Hollingsworth, *The Asians in East Africa*, pg. 54.

[72] J.S. Mangat, *A History of The Asians in East Africa*, pg. 27.

While commenting on Gregory's book, *Quest for Equality*, a well-known figure in the East African Asian community said about him, "[he] has emphasized the fact that the Indian immigrants over the last one-hundred years really 'opened up' East and Central Africa for the Capitalist Consumer Society. They did this without any motivation, but they did it efficiently and cost-effectively".[73] This statement, while intended to be an interpretation is so baseless that its bias rusts through. These Indians had plenty of motivation to work with the British. As time elapsed, these 'interior Indians' would enter new, more lucrative sectors of the economy. Mangat tells us that:

> Many of these skilled immigrants were to launch a variety of business enterprises as contractors, outfitters, builders, mechanics, etc, and helped to supplement the activities of the Indian commercial population in East Africa – which also witnessed a steady expansion during this time.[74]

What ultimately occurred was a transition – a transition of land and financial resources. While land was not a key factor in Kenya where the most desirable lands (the white highlands) were reserved for the Europeans, by 1936, Indians in Tanzania owned over 282,843 acres.[75] The Indians were able to purchase these properties since their community as a whole had managed to accumulate a rather healthy capital base both from the operation of small retail shops (dukawallas) and larger trading centers. More crucial

---

73 Robert Gregory, Quest for Equality, foreward vii.

74 J.S. Mangat, *A History of the Asians in East Africa*, pg. 77.

75 L.W. Hollingsworth, *The Asians of East Africa*, pg. 65.

to Indian capital accumulation, however, was the dominant role Indians assumed within the colonial civil service. For example, according to Mangat:

> ...the number of Indian employees in the central and provincial administrations in Kenya, Uganda, and Zanzibar steadily increased. In every department of government – including the ones newly estab-lished-Indians filled the middle ranks in an extensive variety of capacities: as hospital assistants, surveyors, droughtsmen, clerks, cashiers, customs collectors, police-men, artisans, mechanics, carpenters, post and telegraph assistants, shorthand writers, typists, and compounders, etc.[76]

The absolute monopolization of the civil service by Indians over Africans was inevitable in East Africa. European prejudices and preferences favored the Asian in all recruitment processes. Once in, the Indian would make it his duty to simultaneously bring in other Asians while securing his own course of promotion. Operating in a colonial environment, which is by definition a zero- sum world, he would overtly thwart black attempts at advancement. Nizar Motani discusses this scenario in his work, *On His Majesty's Services in Uganda: The Origins of Uganda's African Civil Service*. According to Motani:

> ...their [Asians] subordinate status did not prevent them from exercising direct and indirect influence over the policy of

---

[76] J.S. Mangat, *A History of the Asians in East Africa*, pg. 75.

Africanization…Africanization meant the gradual elimination of the Asian clerical service…The Asian clerks countered this threat by demonstrating the excellence of their work to their European superiors and by manipulating the clerical training schemes for Africans which British officers in Uganda were reported to have shown a temporal inability to work with African staff. Indeed, there are indications that a tacit alliance to this end developed between European and Asian staff during the inter-war years…[77]

This report conflicts with the commonly held view as expressed by Gregory that, "the Asians deeply resented the various forms of discrimination implicit in the colonial system".[78] To the contrary, The Asians, quite understandably, were given to preserving the status quo. They must have succumbed to the natural and human instincts for survival, thus keeping the Africans out of a hosts of middle-grade positions.[79]

The facts relayed here are valuable because without them one cannot understand how the Indian presence evolved. The Indian population grew proportionately with the community's overall prestige. Unlike the Africans they conspired to keep out of the public sector, the Indians were

---

[77] Nizar Motani, *On His Majesty's Service in Uganda: The Origins of Uganda's African Civil Service*, 1912-1940 (Syracuse University, New York, 1977), pg. 3.

[78] Robert Gregory, *Quest for Equality*, pg. 22.

[79] Nizar Motani, *On His Majesty's Service in Uganda: The Origins of Uganda's African Civil Service*, 1912-1940, pg. 49.

able to amass a considerable amount of capital and influence. "The growth of the Indian role in East Africa during this period also accounted for the rise of a variety of institutions in the territories".[80] These 'institutions' and the interests that defined them came into conflict with the aspirations of a mobilizing African body as the 1930's came to an end. There is no greater case to draw from to illustrate this point than the independence movement in Kenya.

---

[80] J.S. Mangat, *Asians in East Africa*, pg. 96.

Chapter 5

The Indian as Anti-Uhuru (1940-1963)

It is still asserted by many, especially Indians, that the Asian community played a supportive if not pivotal role in Kenya's fight for independence. It is the purpose of this section to shed light on the truth. It will be forwarded here that not only did the Indian community refuse to assist the black community in its fight for Uhuru (freedom), but that being first and foremost colonizers themselves, sought to prevent independence from occurring at all.

The departure point for any grounded discussion of this nature is to first digest the fact put forth by Gregory that, "for a time the Asians themselves were attracted to the possibility of a transfer of a portion of British East Africa to the government of India for administration as an Indian colony or failing that, an exclusive Asian settlement somewhere in the lowlands".[81] Next, one has to dissect the larger myth of the Indian freedom-fighter into at least two refined myths.

They will be referred to here as the "Nehru myth" and the "organizational myth". The theme of these two myths will be summarized and explicated in real, but brief terms before being joined together and evaluated in the proper context – the State of Emergency of October 1952. The

---

[81] Robert Gregory, *Quest for Equality*, pg. 38.

Emergency will serve in this capacity since it represents the time in history when the anti-colonial movement in Kenya was at its peak. An effort will be made to properly assess the Asian position in this pinnacle moment in Kenyan and East African history.

The first step in debunking the Nehru myth is to show that neither he nor his 'pro-African rhetoric' affected the actions of the Indians in East Africa during the greater portion of his reign (1947-1965). The second step is to show that the Indian communities in Kenya, as colorful and interesting as they were, identified first and foremost with the white man.

On Nehru and Africa, Padma Srivastava states the following:

> To him Africa was not a dark continent. It had a rich history and culture. It was a continent of contrast, conflict, challenge and change. In his words 'And people not knowing all this history have talked about it as if it had no past, no background and no culture. I hope that people will get to know more about it'. India under Nehru's leadership was the first country to come out strongly in support of the struggles for freedom in various countries of Africa.[82]

Nelson Mandela has said, "India became the beloved spokesperson of the voiceless masses not only of our country and Namibia, but of the people like ours throughout

---

[82] Padma Srivastava, 'Jawahar Nehru's Perception of Africa' *India Quarterly* July-September 1996 (Vol. LII, no.3), pg. 21.

the world".[83] One can easily be led to accept the Nehru myth. The words of Mandela certainly imply that the 'pro-African' stance assumed by Nehru was part of some positive force that swept through the continent. Srivastava notes correctly that Nehru as India's leader, "repeatedly advised Indians to identify themselves with Africans because they were both victims of the same policy of apartheid and racial discrimination".[84]

However, there exists no proof that the formal position of the Indian government ever materialized into anything of worth on the ground between the Indian colonizers and the blacks they were exploiting in the immediate pre-independence era. Sadly, the great Nehru was paid little attention by Indians. N.S. Carey Jones offers an analysis of the situation as it took shape in Kenya.

> The Indian government, after Indian independence, abandoned its role of protecting Indian interests in Kenya. As a country which had itself attained independence in Kenya as a simple proposition. It seems to have assumed that it could best look after Indians in Kenya by supporting African 'nationalists' and advising the Indian community in Kenya to identify themselves with movements for independence.

He continues:

---

[83] Padama Srivastava, 'Jawahar Nehru's Perception of Africa', pg. 96.

[84] Padama Srivastava, 'Jawahar Nehru's Perception of Africa', pg. 27.

> This was a pious and unrealistic policy...
> the policy ignored reality in that Kenyan
> Asians were themselves a privileged group.
> They were higher socially than Africans.
> They had status, if less than the highest.
> They enjoyed a higher standard of living
> than they could hope to enjoy in India. [85]

The point to be made here is strait forward. While
Nehru might have been a great man who harbored a sincere
desire to see Africans achieve freedom it is of no concern
because his people in the East African colonies did not.

Crucial to understanding the primary fallacy of the
organizational pressure myth is realizing the need to sepa-
rate the actions of individual Indian activists from those of
the Indian activist organizations. For example, an Indian
named M.A. Desai was a political ally to Harry Thuku,
the founder of the radical Kikuyu Central Association.[86]
Another Indian, Isher Dass, accompanied Jomo Kenyatta
to London to make demands on the British colonial government in 1929.[87] Famous trade union organizer, Makhan
Singh, opened up his East Africa Worker's Federation to
Africans and eventually spent over eleven years in detention
during British rule.

The organization pressure myth is based on the assertion that the various organizations erected by Indians
from the inter-war years onward directly aided the Kenyan
cause for independence. The main error of the propagators
of this myth is the assumption that the acts of the high-

---

[85] N.S. Carey Jones, *The Anatomy of Uhuru*, pgs. 96-97.

[86] Dana Seidenberg, *Uhuru and the Kenyan Indians*, pg. 16.

[87] Robert Gregory, *Quest for Equality*, pg. 42.

lighted individuals were representative of the larger Indian community.

In truth, the acts of the aforementioned brazen Indians were aberrations from the norm and largely offset by the constant anti-black position assumed by the formal organizations. For example, Isher Dass, after lending his support to an initiative designed to prevent Asian domination of the various economic sectors by curbing Asian immigration was met with repeated protest and eventually assassinated by angered Indian folk.[88] Likewise, A.B. Patel, considered by Gregory to be the "foremost Indian politician during the colonial years"[89] was wishy-washy at best.

While claiming to be pro-African, Patel disassociated himself and the Indian National Congress from the actions of Singh and even intimated to the British that he was receiving support from the communists abroad.[90] Patel's conservatism was truly representative of the Indian community's position as a whole. As Seidenberg writes, "the Asians continued to take a middle-of –the-road stand – continuing to oppose certain settler policies but never fully aligning themselves with the African leaders"[91] This type of Indian ambiguity, which caused Indian organizations to be largely ineffective in helping blacks achieve progress, eventually sharpened into a position of blatant hostility as independence grew nearer.

The Emergency of 1952 was provoked by a period of political violence labeled Mau Mau by the British. Mau Mau was a predominantly Kikuyu movement. This is

---

[88] Dana Seidenberg, *Uhuru and the Kenyan Indians*, pg. 26.

[89] Robert Gregory, *Quest for Equality*, pg. 13.

[90] Robert Gregory, *Quest for Equality*, pg. 74.

[91] Dana Seidenberg, *Uhuru and the Kenyan Indian*, pg. 134.

understandable when one considers that it was primarily the Kikuyu's land, the Highlands, which became the major area of focus for the settlers. The Kikuyu "rebels" would eventually come to call themselves the Land and Freedom Army. Donald Barnett and Karari Njama attempt to describe the effect that the European settler had on the displaced Kikuyu.

> It is not only the brute fact of landlessness, land hunger and insecurity of tenure which conditioned Kikuyu involvement in the nationalist movement and peasant revolt; it is also the fact that for a people who attach such sacred meaning to the land areas alienated within their field of expertise, unattainable yet in considerable measure unused by its new owners.[92]

The effects of European settlement would prove catastrophic.

> By 1934, some 6,543,360 acres of land had been alienated for occupation by 2,027 settlers; an average of 2,534 acres per occupant, of which only 274 acres were actually under cultivation...By 1952, some 9,000 settlers held exclusive rights to 16,700 square mile of land...while several million Africans sought to eke out a liveli-

---

[92] Donald Barnett and Karari Njami, *Mau Mau from Within* (Monthly Review, New York, 1996), pg. 34.

hood within their increasingly congested reserves.[93]

By the time of the Emergency, Kenya was indeed a lovely country to be a non-African".[94] If you were a Kikuyu, however, you had many legitimate grievances. As Josiah Kariuki reflected:

> ...with an ever-increasing population, the shortage of land became chronic and our landless young men found themselves working at miserable wages on enormous farms which their fathers owned and were now bringing huge houses and Jaguar cars to European strangers.[95]

Now that the objective depravity of the Kikuyu people approaching the Emergency has been established it is expedient to locate the Indian within the crisis. At the time the Mau Mau movement, Indians in Bombay were still basking in the glory of their new freedom granted by the British. One must be curious as to what Indians in Nairobi were doing? The facts reveal that they were becoming more and more anti-Kikuyu, anti-Kenyan and anti-independence. Speaking of Indian 'activists' and their contributions to Africans, Apa Pant patronizingly ponders:

---

[93] Donald Barnett and Karari Njami, *Mau Mau from With*in, pg. 32.

[94] Fred Majdalany, *State of Emergency*, (Houghton, Boston, 1963), pg. 21.

[95] Josiah Mwangi Kariuki, Mau Mau Detainee (Penguin, Baltimore, 1963), pg. 42.

> ...I wonder whether they could really
> communicate their message to the African
> who, encased in his own tribal forms of be-
> haviour and often exhibiting, as in the case
> of Mau Mau, an atavistic (nowadays called
> fundamentalists) response to the rapidly
> changing environment around him, could
> have hardly listened to them.[96]

Pant's position is hardly shocking. Carl Rosenberg, Jr. and John Nottingham have found that Mau Mau was interpreted by many Europeans to be the "product of the Kikuyu people's inability to adapt to the demands of rapid modernization".[97] In reality, the story of the Land and Freedom Army is not about modernization at all, but about a genocide campaign and a people's attempt to survive it. What Pant and other Indians refuse to acknowledge is that the Mau Mau revolt itself was instigated by the colonial government's refusal to permit African political channels to flow freely.

As mentioned earlier, Harry Thuku founded the first viable political organization in 1921 called the East African Association. By 1922, Thuku was imprisoned by the British for his role in the group. While Thuku's arrest was sup-ported by the moderates of another African organization - the Kikuyu Association – the masses of the people sup-ported him fully. Over 7,000 Kenyans showed up at the

---

[96] Robert Gregory, *Quest for Equality*, foreward ix.

[97] Carl Rosenberg, Jr. and John Nottingham, *The Myth of Mau Mau: Nationalism in Kenya* (Hoover Institution, California, 1966), pg. 16.

site of his detention to protest his imprisonment.[98] One of the protestors was one Mary Muthani Nyanjiru who at one point during the demonstration "leapt to her feet and shouted to the men: 'you take my dress and give me your trousers. You men are cowards. What are you waiting for? Our leader is in there. Let's get him'".[99] Subsequently, several natives would be killed, including Nyanjiru. The violence would lead to the deportation of Thuku and the dissolving of the organization.

Another organization, The Kenya Central Association, was founded in 1925 to carry on with advocating "African initiatives". Jomo Kenyatta, the future Kenyan president, became the entity's general secretary and was vocal in calling for land reforms. According to Norman Miller, "politically, by 1939 the KCA had emerged as the main organization of African protest". The KCA boasted a paid membership of 2,000 persons and even more supporters. However, the organization was outlawed and forced to go underground by the start of World War II.[100]

Ultimately, it was the deportation of Thuku and the disbarment of the KCA that pushed the Kikuyu politicization process into disorganization. As the war came to a close, Eliud Mathu founded the Kenyan African Union in 1944, but little real change took place. That is, no land had changed hands, nor had any additional privileges been granted to the squatters [farm laborers] and farmers. As Kariuki recalled, "normal political methods through

---

[98] Carl Rosenberg, Jr. and John Nottingham, *The Myth of Mau Mau: Nationalism in Kenya*, pg. 51.

[99] Carl Rosenberg, Jr. and John Nottingham, *The Myth of Mau Mau: Nationalism in Kenya*, pg. 51-52.

[100] Josiah Mwangi Kariuki, *Mau Mau Detainee*, pgs. 19-30.

the KAU seemed to be getting nowhere".[101] For example, a major petition submitted to the British Government by the KAU was described simply as immature..."[102] In short, Mau Mau was the last resort. It was the military part or phrase of an embattled political movement grounded in easily identifiable economic grievances. Yet, the majority of Asians (conservatives and most moderates) were anxious to restore 'order' in the colony and became actively involved in Emergency measures to suppress Mau Mau.[103]

The Land and Freedom Army was aware that the Indian community was against them from the beginning. The Indian had helped to implement a system of permits which according to Frank Furedi, "had made it difficult for squatters to send their produce back to the reserves." Consequently, says Furedi, "the squatter was forced to sell to Asian traders..." In 1948, squatters and farmers boycotted Asian traders out of protest after the Indians collectively decided to dramatically reduce the going price for potatoes. The boycott spread all over the Highlands and leaders of the KCA and Mau Mau group traveled around the settled areas to spread the campaign.[104] This is just one example of many. During the Emergency, "all the major Asian political organizations, including the Congress and the Federation of Indian Chambers of Commerce and Industry, pledged loyalty to the government".[105] In addition, A.B. Patel and

---

[101] Josiah Mwangi Kariuki, *Mau Mau Detainee*, pg. 49.

[102] Carl Rosenberg, Jr. and John Nottingham, *The Myth of Mau Mau: Nationalism in Kenya*, pg. 220.

[103] Dana Seidenberg, *Uhuru and the Kenyan Indian*, pg. 112.

[104] Frank Furedi, *The Mau Mau War in Perspective* (Ohio University, Ohio, 1989), pgs. 43 & 107.

[105] Robert Gregory, *Quest for Equality*, pg. 81.

the Indian National Conference supported a government proposal or settlement under "which settlers would continue to enjoy exclusive control of the Highlands, among other things".[106] The proposal, called the Lyttelton Plan, was flatly rejected by Africans who were dismayed at the fact that they had not even been consulted by the government. Mathu charged that the Asians had joined the settlers and the government in "a conspiracy against Africans". No one could debate this since Indians could be seen volunteering themselves for the suppression squads which terrorized Kikuyu communities during the crisis.[107]

Colin Leys found it understandable why Asians, "with few exceptions...stood aloof from the African leaders' attempts to reduce European dominance".[108] So did Elizabeth Hopkins who is quoted by Ghai and Ghai speaking of the Mau Mau Emergency and its meaning to the Indian. She writes:

> ...Politically ...the Indians were to identify with the government, not with the African resurgents, for they felt that their position would be threatened if the movement proved successful. In this commitment to the colonial superstructure, they were ironically to find themselves in opposition...[109]

As Gregory points out, from 1954-1958, perhaps the most important four years in its history, the Indian

---

[106] Dana Seidenberg, *Uhuru and the Kenyan Indians*, pg. 132.

[107] Robert Gregory, *Quest for Equality*, pgs. 82-84.

[108] Colin Leys, *Underdevelopment in Kenya: The Political Economy of Neocolonialism*, (University of California, Berkely, 1975), pg. 45.

[109] Dharam and Yash Ghai, *A Portrait of a Minority*, pgs. 82-83.

National Congress was dominated by J.S Mangat.[110] In his 1956 Presidential address to the Congress, Mangat stated his conviction that:

> ...There is no influence so potent as self-interests; and our self-interest ordains that we should be in favor of the perpetuation of the British connection in this country.[111]

One Ismali found the sight of opportunistic Indians scurrying like funky bandits unbearable. He looked to a group of his fellows and lamented over the moral defeat they had suffered by supporting the British. He said: "time is not on our side. Unless we act, history will brand us traitors to this country".[112] The Indian was a traitor not only to Kenya, but to all of black East Africa. In 1955, when Julius Nyere traveled from Tanzania to New York to present his case for independence, the Governor of the colony sent Iqbal Chand Chopra, a Punjabi Hindu, to "state before the United Nations that, from the Asians' view, the country would not be ready for independence in another twenty-five years."[113]

The point here is simple. The Indian never wanted the African to experience freedom because he was stuck to the imperial structure like a baby to its mother's perched nipple. It can be stated objectively that the entire colonial experience in East Africa amounted to an opportunity for the Indian. One that he milked greedily. Zarwan contends

---

[110] Robert Gregory, *Quest for Equality*, pg. 83.

[111] Dharam and Yash Ghai, *A Portrait of a Minority*, pg. 82.

[112] Dana Seidenberg, *Uhuru and the Kenyan Indians*, pg. 132.

[113] Robert Gregory, *Quest for Equality*, pg. 109.

that, "Indian access to capital, through the credit system and reinvestment of profits is crucial to understanding their success".[114] In the next section, examining patterns of Indian capital accumulation and manipulation of the relevant political and economic institutions in particular, will help to explain Indian success as well as African failure after Kenyan independence was attained in 1963.

---

[114] John Zarwan, *Indian Businessmen in Kenya During the Twentieth Century: A Case Study*, pg. 217.

Chapter 6

The Indian as a
Neo-Colonizer (1963-2000)

National liberation exists when, and only
when, the national productive forces, have
been freed from all forms of foreign domination.[115]

A layman would surely figure: the best reason not to do
something again is because it failed the first time. The logic
is evident enough. However, one hopes that persons dedi-
cated to finding solutions to pressing problems involving
people and issues of human dignity would be willing to
go slightly further. For example, the Africanist of today,
when considering 'Africanization', should ask how and why
it failed in East Africa. The fact that it failed in and of itself
is not sufficient reason to discard the initiative or the ideas
behind it.

Africanization meant the "...the gradual elimination of

---

[115] B.A. Ogot and W.R. Ochieng, *Decolonization and Independence
in Kenya* (Ohio University, Athens, 1995), pg. 85.

the Asian clerical service..." and other state operations.[116] The Africanization experiment and its failure is commonly used as rationale for keeping the Indian in his position of relative dominance and the African in his position of dependence. For instance, in his book [cited earlier], Himbara writes, "the Africanization attempts failed, reflecting the fact that those who acquired businesses possessed neither the skills nor capital to hold their own in the market place".[117] As this statement implies, the book serves to glorify the Indian or 'Kenyan capitalist' for his own business acumen and capacity to contribute to overall development.

The focus of this section will be on the Kenyan capitalist as proposed by Himbara. First, however, Africanization as a post-colonial policy measure will not be merely assumed as Himbara does, but configured along the lines of actual developments. Again, it is essential to address the Himbara argument because it ultimately discards any pro-African course of action. When Himbara's crude biases and pseudo-hypothesis regarding Africanization are put aside, a valid examination of the Indian will be possible.

At the time of independence, it was relatively easy to identify the challenges that laid before the African in relation to his Indian counterpart. J.F. Lipscomb summarized them.

> The whole subject of Asian competition with Africans is complicated by the fact that in so many spheres of activity the rising African is now finding his way blocked

---

[116] Nizar Motani, *On His Majesty's Service in Uganda: The Origins of Uganda's African Civil Service*, 1912-1940, pg. 3.

[117] David Himbara, *Kenyan Capitalists, the State, and Development*, pg. 10.

by the Asian. The spheres of activity of the Asian community are wide, but they can also be clearly demarcated. They lie in the professional and commercial worlds, in government and railway service, and in those artisan activities in which more skill and reliability is needed than can yet be secured from any but a few exceptional Africans. The operative word in the previous sentence is the word 'yet', and it remains to be seen whether in time to come Africans will be able to oust Asians from their places in these spheres...But there is no doubt in either African or European minds that the Asians are increasingly blocking the African's path to economic progress and to a higher standard of living.[118]

Under Jomo Kenyatta, the first government of independent Kenya attempted to oust the Asians from their places in the crucial 'spheres' by erecting state mechanisms to become the "architects of private sector African capitalism", or to consolidate themselves as "viable instruments of state capitalism".[119] The program installed to achieve this objective was called Africanization and was intended to place Kenya's black Africans into the center of commercial activity in their own communities. As Ogot and Ochieng explain:

---

[118] J.F. Lipscomb, *White Africans* (Faber and Faber Limited, London, 1955), pg. 123.

[119] David Himbara, "The Failed Africanization of Commerce and Industry in Kenya", *World Development* (Vol. 22, No.3), pg. 469.

> 'Africanization', in particular, was one of the most emotive political slogans in the tumult before independence...Thus, after independence one of the most urgent and pressing problems was to break the foreigners' dominance of the Kenyan economy and transfer it to the Kenyan's.[120]

In Kenya, a disproportionate amount of 'Africanized' business entities ended up in the hands of a particular ethnic group, the Kikuyu. The majority of Kenyans did not benefit from the transfer of power.[121] This has long been one of the major criticisms made against the Kenyatta regime. As Joel Barkan writes, "By the time Moi came into power, the Kikuyu were depicted as malevolent beneficiaries of an undue share of economic growth during the Kenaytta years. In the heat of political mobilization, no distinction was made between what Kikuyu had earned on merit and what they had been given through political patronage".[122] Upon entering office, Moi would displace Kikuyu from key bureaucratic positions in order to solidify his own network of ethnic support.

Needless to say, the program of Africanization failed. The type of transfer spoken of above never occurred. As

---

[120] B.A. Ogot and W.R. Ochieng, *Decolonization and Independence in Kenya,* pg. 85.

[121] The Kikuyu ethnic group comprises 22% of the Kenyan population, compared to: Luhya – 14%; Luo-13%; Kalenjin-12%; Kamba-11%; Meru-6%; Kisii-6%; other African-15%; other (including Asian, European, and Arab) – 1%. Source: 1999 ABC-CLIO, Inc. *Kaleidoscope,* Country: Kenya.

[122] Joel Barkan, *Beyond Capitalism vs. Socailism in Kenya and Tanzania* (Eds) (Lynne Reiner, Boulder, 1994.

already highlighted, the ethnic politics of the public sector overlapped and interfered with the developing private sector during the reign of both Kenyatta's and his successor Moi's reign. Africanization, which was supposed to be a national vehicle for development, deteriorated into a program of elite and ethnic squabbling. As Himbara correctly assesses in his article, 'The Failed Africanization of Commerce and Industry in Kenya', the fragmented nature of the Kenyan governing elite created serious discontinuities in policy implementation. Operating in an ethnically and regionally divided environment, the groups in control of the state sought to consolidate themselves by empowering a supportive African business class from within their own ethnic ranks."[123]

Himbara's assessment that the failure of Africanization reflects "the fact that those who acquired businesses possessed neither the skills nor capital to hold their own in the market place",[124] does not withstand serious scrutiny. It does not fit the real case of Africanization. That is, the failure of Africanization seems to reflect more the dysfunctional dynamics of a new and aspiring state than it does the value and indispensability of the Indian capitalist. For example, the Trade Licensing Act of 1967, which was designed to limit the trading activities of non-citizens was never enforced. True 'support' was never provided to the majority of prospective Kenyan investors at all, but only those within ethnic circles. Thus, the program never gained speed and the state never developed the momentum to

---

[123] David Himbara, "The Failed Africanization of Commerce and Industry in Kenya", *World Development* (Vol. 22, No. 3), pgs. 469-470.

[124] David Himbara, *Kenyan Capitalist, the State and Development*, pgs. 63-64.

support it. Himbara admits this and even provides evidence of Indian defiance of the newly invoked law.

> There is, in effect, further evidence to illustrate the fact that the Kenyan state was merely playing lip service to its Africanization policies, having long recognized that it neither possessed the power nor the will to force foreign and domestic large scale Indian manufactures to appoint African distributors. For example, in 1967, perturbed by the "exceedingly disappointing" rate of progress in the appointment of African distributors by manufacturers, the Kenyan Government stated that "strong warning is given that actions designed to frustrate Government's efforts should be avoided as much as possible...More than half a decade later, in August 1973, the manufacturing sector was reminded that the government: *has indicated to you its determination that the distribution of locally manufactured products should be passed on to Africans as quickly as possible.*

Himbara continues:

> It is worth emphasizing that the Kenyan state was very aware of the limits of its power vis-a-vis the manufactures. Its rhetoric was essentially for public consumption...Meanwhile, the state continued to engage in a make-believe exercise that gave the impression that the Africanization of

commerce and industry was still being im-
plemented. For example, in 1980, the state
issued yet another "threat" to Kenyan-
Based manufactures: *As you are well aware,
the Government has decided that the distri-
bution of essential commodities will in the
future be done through citizen distributors
only. In the exercise of appointing their distributors...manufactures are expected to work
in close liaison and consultation with this
Ministry.*[125]

Still, Himbara is determined to use the experience of
Africanization, a process which by his own analysis never
truly occurred, as evidence that the Indian capitalist is a su-
perman, and that he is destined to rule the 'crucial spheres'
of Kenyan society. The argument is weak. Where he attempts to show the futility and silliness of trying to replace
Indians with Africans in a society where Indians have historically ran the economy, he only shows that Africanization
was never really given half-a-chance. Where he embarks to
portray the Indian as the only credible force within the private sector, he only shows that the Kenyan coolie turned
capitalist played an undeniably instrumental role in seeing
this African initiative flounder by refusing to employ and
include Africans in the operations of state and private commercial trade outfits.

Himbara adds insult to injury by attempting to ste-
reotype the African entrepreneurs who by and large were
neglected by both the Kenyatta and Moi regimes. He attributes the failures of the 'African entrepreneur' to his culture

---

[125] David Himbara, *Kenyan Capitalists, the State, and Development*,
pgs. 63-64.

which of course is opposite to that of the Indian. Himbara is able to make such a cultural argument because of his assumption that inherent in Kenyan Indians is some amount of business acumen. Himbara is not willing to grant any credence to the claim that the Indian has achieved economic predominance primarily due to his structurally superior position over the black African during the colonial period. This is certainly an interesting argument when we consider the fact that the Oshwals (Shahs), the most prominent Indian group in Kenya today, were historically a subsistence farming community in their native India.[126] We should recall Gregory's description:

> Most of the Asians were thus drawn to East Africa by a hope of rising above the poverty level. The peasant farmers, who comprised most of the immigrants were fortunate to feed their families, and many left homes without ever having owned a pair of shoes.[127]

Michael Chege finds even more fault with Himbara's thesis. In his written response to Himbara he provides a portrayal of the Kenyan capitalist that is much less flattering. Addressing the assertion forwarded by Himbara and others that Indian manufacturing activity is the engine that has driven Kenya since independence, Chege replies:

> For Kenya, it is worth noting that most expansion in the industrial and consumer

---

[126] John Zarwan, *Indian Businessman in Kenya During the Twentieth Century: A Case Study*, pg. 13.

[127] Robert Gregory, *The Quest for Equality*, pg. 6.

goods sector – 69 percent of manufacturing output between 1964 and 1984 – was derived from domestic demand in the captive African consumer sector in agriculture... Yet in the interests of import substitution, the Kenya government...instituted a range of policies – a moderately over-valued exchange rate, quantitative import controls, high import tariffs on consumer goods, low capital goods taxation, sub-market interest rates, and fiscal subsidies – all with the goal of stimulating local manufacturing. In an economy with only two categories of tradeables, farm goods and manufactures, these policy instruments penalized agriculture to the same extent that they subsidized industry.[128]

In other words, from 1964 to 1984, black farmers were supporting the same Indian run manufacturing sector that was supposedly supporting them. Even more interesting is Chege's evidence that the Indian run manufacturing sector is attaining its profit margins not from cost-efficient production, but through efficient corruption. Here he reports on the World Bank's thwarted effort to help spawn economical development in Kenya:

World Bank efforts to dismantle this structure and replace it with a more internationally-competitive one in the 1980's and

---

[128] Michael Chege, Introducing Race as a Variable Into the Political Economy of Kenya Debate: An Incendiary Idea, *Africa Affairs* (97, 1998), pg. 222.

1990's met little success. This is because, as a Bank study in 1994 remarked, *'the uneasy relationship between Asian-Kenyan entrepreneurs and African Kenyans in political power created a highly protected, uncompetitive and oligopolistic industrial structure'.* These 'sweetheart deals' are the opposite of the antagonistic tendencies of the Moi state to the Kikuyu and to the export-crop agriculture; and the fierce manner in which kinship-based cartels sought to protect their privileges in the face of economic liberalization in the 1990's should not be underestimated.

To hammer home his point, he continues:

Then there is the ultimate irony. Contrary to the supposed Africa ineptitude, the spectacular binge of early 1990's multinational take-overs, involving Union Carbide, Marshalls Motor Company, Twentieth Century Fox, Firestone International, etc, by a group of Kenyan Asians in alliance with top Kalenjin politicians, using commandeered state resources, are proudly paraded as 'the latest trend in (Kenya Indian) patterns of accumulation' to illustrate Asian business acumen'.[129]

---

[129] Michael Chege, Introducing Race as a Variable Into the Political Economy of Kenyan Debate: An Incendiary Idea, *Africa Affairs*, pgs. 223-225.

The Indian at times resorted to blunt theft. At the center of Kenya's infamous Goldenberg scandal was an Indian named Kamlesh Pattni. Pattni was charged with stealing 13.5 billion shillings in a series of fraudulent transactions, one involving the now defunct Exchange Bank Ltd.[130]

Again, it is important to realize that this type of Indian behavior was not inimitable to Kenya. Phares Mutibwa provides insight into the true role of the Indian capitalist as it manifested in Uganda during Milton Obote's second regime. He reports:

> Another element which Obote's regime introduced in the game of economic plunder was the Asian community, who now became important in the manipulation of the economy. They became the regime's agents, the linch pins of the whole system of economic exploitation; most of the money exported from the country went through the hands of some Asians whose return the regime engineered.

Asian firms were thus enabled to borrow money from government financial institutions without firm guarantees for its return. The largest single loan, issued at Obote's direction and guaranteed by him in writing in his capacity as minister of Finance, amounted to 14.7 billion shillings (old currency).[131]

---

130 Catherine Bond, "Businessman Deported Amid Kenyan Corruption Scandal," *CNN*, August 28, 1999. [Online] http://www.cnn.com/WORLD/africa/9908/28/kenya.corruption/

131 Phares Mutibwa, *Uganda Since Independence*, pg. 154.

Foreign exchange activities provided new opportunities for Ugandan Indians. Mutibwa continues:

> In a move intended to attract foreign exchange and preserve what little is in the country, the government instituted the Forex Bureaux, which are free to buy and sell foreign currency at the market rates. While this new policy has enabled Ugandans working abroad to repatriate their money, the system has fallen short of intentions behind it since those who appear to benefit most from it are foreigners. The people who attract most criticism are the Asians, most of whom have been allowed to return and reclaim the property confiscated from them by Amin; they are alleged to be more interested in buying U.S. currency and British pounds than in selling such currency to the local people, and to be once again 'milking the Ugandan cow rather than feeding it'.[132]

The Indian's ability to usurp profits from the types of transactions described above has only enhanced his capacity to expand and dominate vital industries. Since the collapse of the East African Common Market in 1977, studies reveal that the role of the Kenyan Indian capitalist has expanded to spectacular proportions. It also notes that "nearly all large-scale industrial undertakings since the late 1970's were traceable to local Indians". Similarly, "most of the divested enterprises were acquired by Kenyan Indian

---

[132] Phares Mutibwa, *Uganda Since Independence*, pg. 194.

capitalists".[133] Likewise, the implementation of certain International Monetary Fund (IMF) Structural Adjustment Policies (SAPs) has provided clear advantages to Asians over the African businessman. Below, Joel Barkan provides an example of Indian foul play from Tanzania.

> The failure of Adjustment to provide for basic services, particularly education, has offended many Tanzanians, including members of the intelligentsia who, though highly critical of Nyere's policies, applauded his commitment to providing basic social services for all Tanzanians.

Economic liberalization moreover, has clearly favored some Tanzanians over others...Liberalization of exchange control has also favored those traders and private manufacturers who can best take advantage of the new rules – in this case, members of Tanzania's urban-based Asian community rather than would-be African entrepreneurs... Asians have now capitalized on the new system...[134]

Even at this point, there remains one more myth to discard. Many argue that the income of Indians somehow benefits the society indirectly, either through tax revenue to the state or some type of nebulous reinvestment into the local community. Unfortunately, this often does not occur. As Gregory admits in his South Asian in East Africa, "… the Asians through their long history in East Africa sent

---

[133] David Himbara, "Failed Africanization of Commerce and Industry in Kenya", *World Development,* pg. 470.

[134] Joel Barkan, Beyond Capitalism vs. Socialism in Kenya & Tanzania, pg. 30.

considerable sums overseas".[135] He continues, "One knowledgeable individual has estimated that nearly 50 per cent of the Asians' profits left East Africa".[136] This is bad enough. What is even more disheartening, however, is the fact that the little money that Indians did keep in East Africa (excluding any capital reinvestments) often ended up being delivered as bribes to former President Moi,[137] a man Human Rights Watch charged with sponsoring ethnic violence to maintain power.[138]

---

[135] Robert Gregory, *South Asian in East Africa* (Westview, Boulder, 1993), pg. 329.

[136] Robert Gregory, *South Asians in East Africa*, pgs. 338-339.

[137] Joel Barkan, *Beyond Capitalism vs. Socialism in Kenya & Tanzania*, pg. 86.

[138] See Human Rights Watch, *Divide and Rule* (Human Rights Watch, New York, 1993).

Chapter 7

Conclusion

What can be said of the Indian? What can the Indian say for himself? The International Organization for Drug Control for 1996 has charted the increase of cocaine entering the African continent. Indians have been implicated as the organizers. Mandrax and metaqualone from India penetrates the whole of East and Southern Africa, and there have been cases of metaqualone being manufactured in Mozambique, where a laboratory was destroyed in 1995.[139] This suggests that with time the Indian will find more lucrative ways of exploiting the weaknesses of developing African societies. Perhaps by playing a role in the increasing importation and illegal dumping of toxic waste from European companies.[140]

At best, the Indian in East Africa has shown himself to be an interesting, dynamic and accomplished parasite. Financing the slave trade and formulating strategies for its expansion. Later, he would put his foot in the way of the

---

[139] The Indian Ocean Newsletter, "Drug Circuits", March 15, 1997.

[140] "Somalia Appeals for Help to Clean Up Hazardous Waste", *The East African Standard* [Nairobi] March 5, 2005. [online] http://allafrica.com/stories/200503070756.html

black as he attempted to cross the threshold of independence, coldly calculating his potential loss as his own homeland of India celebrated its new found freedom. Today, he sits at his desk with his black maid working for mere maize in the background waiting for another African run enterprise to collapse so that he can purchase and refurbish it with illicit state funds. Still, we find him keeping his books and contemplating his possibilities in terms of African tragedies. The Indian has made political and economic development impossible. Albert Memmi's words seem to be so fitting: "The mere existence of the colonizer creates oppression…" [141]

It has been proposed here that the Indian is an enemy to the black humans of East Africa.

---

[141] Albert Memmi, *The Colonizer and the Colonized*, pg. 150.

Bibliography

ABC-CLIO, Inc. 1999 – *Kaleidoscope.*

Ake, Claude, *Democracy and Development in Africa* (The Brookings Institution, Washington, DC 1996).

Ani, Marimba, *Yurugu: An African Centered Critique of European Cultural Thought and Behavior* (Africa World Press, Trenton, 1994).

Ayittey, George, *Africa Betrayed* (St. Martin's Press, New York, 1992).

Barkan, Joel, *Beyond Capitalism vs. Socialism in Kenya and Tanzania* (Eds) (Lynne Reiner, Boulder, 1994.

Barnett, Donald and Karari Njami, *Mau Mau from Within* (Monthly Review, New York, 1996).

Barrat Brown, Michael, *Africa's Choices* (Penguin Books, London, 1995).

Bharati, A., *The Asians in East Africa: Jayhind and Uhuru* (Nelson-Hall Company, Chicago, 1972).

Bond, Catherine, "Businessman Deported Amid Kenyan Corruption Scandal," *CNN*, August 28, 1999. [Online] http://www.cnn.com/WORLD/africa/9908/28/kenya.corruption/

Carey Jones, N.S., *The Anatomy of Uhuru* (Manchester University, Manchester, 1966).

Chazan, N.Z., *Politics and Society in Contemporary Africa* (Lynne Reinner, Boulder, 1998).

Chege, Michael, Introducing Race as a Variable Into the Political Economy of Kenya Debate: An Incendiary Idea, *Africa Affairs* (97, 1998).

Chege, Michael "The State and Economic Reform in Africa: A Review Article," *African Studies Quarterly.* 4(3): 3. 2000. [Online] URL: http://web.africa.ufl.edu/asq/v4/v4i3a3.htm

Daily Graphic, Reuters. 'World Bank Urged to Check Corruption'. (Ghanaian Newspaper), July 18, 1998

Davidson, Basil, *The African Past*, (Grosset & Dunlap, New York, 1964).

Delf, George, Asians *in East Africa* (Oxford University, London, 1963).

Dotson, Floyd & Lillian, *The Indian Minority of Zambia, Rhodesia and Malawi* (Yale University, New Haven, 1968).

East African Standard, "Somalia Appeals for Help to Clean Up Hazardous Waste", [Nairobi] March 5, 2005.

[Online] http://allafrica.com/stories/200503070756. html

Furedi, Frank, The *Mau Mau War in Perspective* (Ohio University, Ohio, 1989).

Gandhi, M.K. *Satyagraha in South Africa* (Navajivan, Indian, 1928).

Ghai, Dharam and Yash, *A Portrait of a Minority* (University Press, Nairobi, 1970).

Giacomo, Carol, "World Bank Corruption May Top $100 Billion", Reuters May 13, 2004. [Online] http://www.globalpolicy.org/socecon/bwi-wto/wbank/2004/0513corrupt.htm

Gilpin, Robert, 'The Nature of the Economy', C. Roe Goddard, John Passe Smith and John Conklin, *International Political Economy* (eds) (Lynne Reinner, Boulder, 1996).

Gregory, Robert, *India and East Africa: A History of Race Relations Within the British Empire* (Claredon, Oxford, 1971).

Gregory, Robert, *South Asian in East Africa* (Westview, Boulder, 1993).

Gregory, David, *The Quest for Equality* (Orient Longman, New Delhi, 1993).

Himbara, David, "The Failed Africanization of Commerce

and Industry in Kenya", *World Development* (Vol. 22, No.3).

Himbara, David, *Kenyan Capitalists, the State, and Development* (Lynne Reiner, Boulder, 1994).

Hollingsworth, L.W., *The Asians of East Africa* (MacMillan and Co., New York, 1960).

Human Rights Watch, *Divide and Rule* (Human Rights Watch, New York, 1993).

Indian Ocean Newsletter, "Drug Circuits", March 15, 1997.

Joshi, P.S., *The Tyranny of Colour* (E.P. & Commercial Printing, Durban, 1942).

Kariuki, Josiah, Mau Mau Detainee (Penguin, Baltimore, 1963).

Leys, Colin, *Underdevelopment in Kenya: The Political Economy of Neocolonialism*, (University of California, Berkeley, 1975).

Lipscomb, J.F., *White Africans* (Faber and Faber Limited, London, 1955).

Lloyd's List, Reuter Textline, 'Political & Civil Unrest; Kenya'. June 2, 1997.

Majdalany, Fred, *State of Emergency*, (Houghton, Boston, 1963).

Mallaby, Sebastian, How Africa Subsidizes U.S. Health Care, *Washington Post*. November 29, 2004.

Mamdani, Mahmood, *Politics and Class Formation in Uganda* (Monthly Review, New York, 1976).

Mangat, J.S., *A History of the Asians in East* Africa (Claredon, Oxford, 1969).

Marsh, Zoe and G.W. Kingsworth, *An Introduction to the History of East Africa* (The University Press, Cambridge, 1957).

Melady, Thomas Patrick Uganda*: The Asian Exiles* (Orbis Books, New York, 1976).

Memmi, Albert, *The Colonizer and the Colonized* (Beacon, Boston, 1991).

Morris, H.S., *The Indians in Uganda* (The University of Chicago, Chicago, 1968).

Motani, Nizar, *On His Majesty's Service in Uganda: The Origins of Uganda's African Civil Service*, 1912-1940 (Syracuse University, New York, 1977).

Mutibwa, Phares, *Uganda Since Independence* (Africa World Press, Trenton, 1992).

Ogot, B.A. and W.R. Ochieng, *Decolonization and Independence in Kenya* (Ohio University, Athens, 1995).

Poliakov, L. 'Racism in Europe', Anthony de Reuck and

Julie Knight, *Caste and Race* (eds.) (J & A Churchill, London, 1967).

Rashidi, Runoko, *African Presence in Early Asia* (Transaction Publishers, London, 1985)

Rosenberg, Jr. Carl, and John Nottingham, *The Myth of Mau Mau: Nationalism in Kenya* (Hoover Institution, California, 1966).

Seidenberg, Dana, *Uhuru and the Kenyan Indians* (Vikas, New Delhi, 1983).

Sorenson, M.P.K., *Origins of White Settlement in Kenya*, (Oxford, London, 1968).

Sowell, Thomas, Race *and Culture* (Basic Books, New York, 1994).

Sowell, Thomas, 'Talents of the Rich Also Benefit the Poor' *Chicago Tribune*, August 20, 1996.

Srivastava, Padma, 'Jawahar Nehru's Perception of Africa' *India Quarterly* July-September 1996 (Vol. LII, no.3).

Strange, Mark, *Cape to Cairo – Rape of a Continent* (Harcourt Brace Jovanovich, New York, 1973).

van de Berghe, Pierre *Race & Racism: A Comparative Perspective* (John Wiley & Sons, New York, 1978).

Wolfers, Michael, *Black Man's Burden Revisited* (St. Martin's, New York, 1974).

Zarwan, John, *Indian Businessmen in Kenya During the Twentieth Century: A Case Study* – Ph.D. Dissertation (Yale University, 1977).

About the Author

Randolph M.K. Joalahliae (1975-) was born to Black parents and raised in southern New Jersey.

He has a Bachelor of Arts Degree from Lincoln University, PA – the nation's first Historically Black College and University (HBCU) - where he became the institution's first graduate to have majored in the field of International Relations. He earned his Master of Arts in International Relations from the Johns Hopkins School of Advanced International Studies (SAIS) in Washington, DC where he concentrated in African Studies and International Economics. He earned his Juris Doctorate Degree from the Georgetown University Law Center in Washington, DC.

The publication of this book was financed by the author. The author has pledged to donate all proceeds earned from the sale of this text to a suitable cause.